CogAT Test Prep Series

NON-VERBAL BATTERY

FIGURE CLASSIFICATION

Grade 2

A step by step STUDY GUIDE

by

MindMine

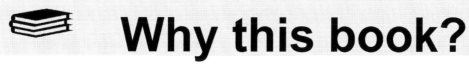 Why this book?

Cognitive abilities test **isn't an IQ test.** Cognitive abilities are brain-based skills related with the mechanisms of learning, memorizing, and paying attention rather than actual knowledge that was learned. **The more you practice, the more you develop** your cognitive flexibility.

- This book is designed to teach concepts and skills in a way kids understand with ease.

- Concepts are taught step by step and introduced incrementally.

- The focus of this book is to provide a solid foundation to fundamental skills. All the skills taught in the book will collectively increase the knowledge and will help kids to prepare and take the test confidently.

- Practice tests that are available in the market may not provide all the concepts needed. **This book is aimed to give both concepts and practice.**

Who should buy this book?

- 2nd graders taking CogAT (Form-7 Level-8)

- 1st graders planning to take CogAT (Any Form)

- 1st, 2nd and 3rd graders seeking to enrich their ANALYTICAL and SPATIAL skills

📚 What is covered?

This book extensively covers **FIGURE CLASSIFICATION** section of **Non-Verbal Battery** Approximately 165 unique questions

📚 2 FULL LENGTH PRACTICE TESTS with Answers

Full Length Practice Test#1	15 Questions
Full Length Practice Test#2	15 Questions

📚 FIGURE CLASSIFICATION

Similar in COLOR	20 Questions
Similar in SHAPE	15 Questions
Similar in NUMBER OF SIDES	15 Questions
Similar in NUMBER OF PARTS (or) FRACTIONAL VALUE	15 Questions
Similar in NUMBER OF FIGURES	20 Questions
SAME or TURNED	30 Questions
LIST OF FEATURES	20 Questions

📚 Table of Contents

Concept	Page#

ANSWERS	Page#

GIFTED & TALENTED

FIGURE CLASSIFICATION

Find the figure that IS MOST SIMILAR TO THE TOP THREE FIGURES

 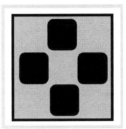 

A **B** **C** **D**

ANSWER: D

FIGURE CLASSIFICATION

HOW TO SOLVE?

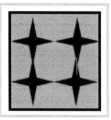 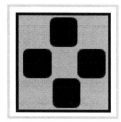 

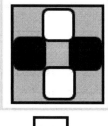  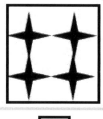 

| A | B | C | D |

STEP#1: Understand how THREE figures are similar. All THREE figures must have something in common.

STEP#2: Find the figure that IS MOST SIMILAR TO THE TOP THREE FIGURES

FIGURE CLASSIFICATION

HOW TO SOLVE?

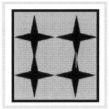  

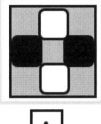   

 A   B   C   D

STEP#1: Understand how THREE figures are similar. All THREE figures must have something in common.

FOUR CONGRUENT BLACK FIGURES INSIDE A GRAY SQUARE.

ANSWER IS "**D**"

STEP#2: Find the figure that IS MOST SIMILAR TO THE TOP THREE FIGURES

"A" IS INCORRECT. NOT ALL FIGURES ARE BLACK

"B" IS INCORRECT. NOT ALL FIGURES ARE SAME SIZE

"C" IS INCORRECT. SQUARE IS NOT GRAY COLOR

"D" IS CORRECT ANSWER

FUNDAMENTAL CONCEPTS

Figures with NO (Zero) Sides

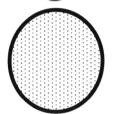   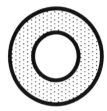

Figures with ONE Side

Figures with TWO Sides

   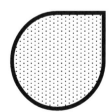

FUNDAMENTAL CONCEPTS

Figures with THREE Sides

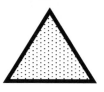   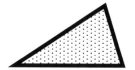

3-sides of
Equal Length

2-sides of
Equal Length

NO-sides of
Equal Length

Figures with THREE Sides

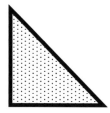   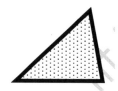   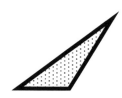

RIGHT Angle
Triangle

ACUTE Angle
Triangle

OBTUSE Angle
Triangle

Figures with FOUR Sides

        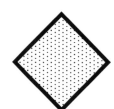   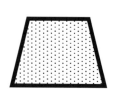

Figures with FOUR Sides

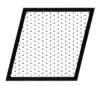 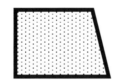  

Figures with FIVE Sides

   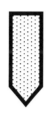

Figures with SIX Sides

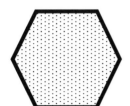  

Figures with SEVEN Sides

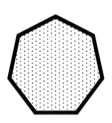 

Figures with EIGHT Sides

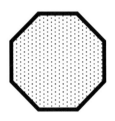 

Figures with NINE Sides

Figures with TEN Sides

Figures with TWELVE Sides

FUNDAMENTAL CONCEPTS

POSITION

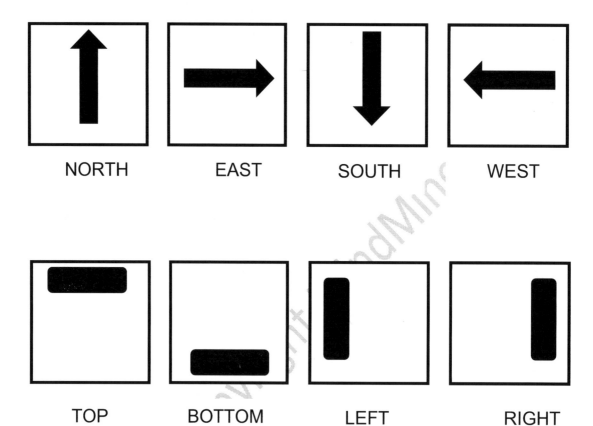

NORTH	EAST	SOUTH	WEST

TOP	BOTTOM	LEFT	RIGHT

CORNER#1	CORNER#2	CORNER#3	CORNER#4

FUNDAMENTAL CONCEPTS

Rotation

CLOCK-WISE

COUNTER CLOCK-WISE

CLOCK-WISE TURN

COUNTER CLOCK-WISE TURN

Pay Attention to the order of colors. When a Figure is turned, ORDER of COLORS remains the same.

Example: For the figure given above, order of colors remains the same when figure is turned clock-wise or counter clock-wise.

Order of Colors:
Black
Gray
White
Dotted Pattern

CONGRUENT SHAPES

Same Shape (Figure) and same size Figures are called congruent.

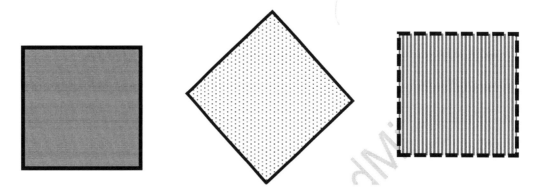

3 squares above are congruent.

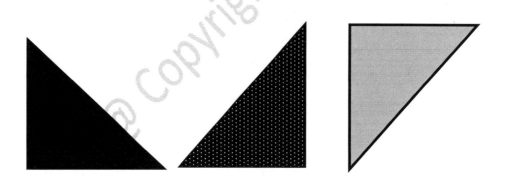

3 Right angled Triangles above are congruent.

COLOR

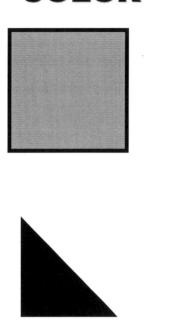 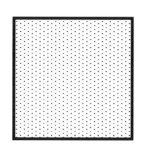 

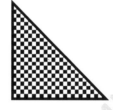 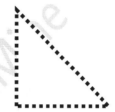

FILL   **PATTERN**   **OUTLINE**

PARTS

   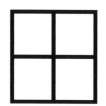

4 -PARTS, NONE SHADED

4 -PARTS, ONE PART SHADED

FRACTIONAL VALUE: 1 OUT OF 4

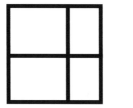

4 -PARTS. BUT NOT ALL ARE OF EQUAL SIZE

PARTS

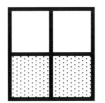 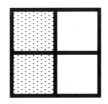 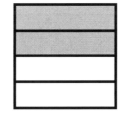

4 -PARTS. 2 PARTS NEXT TO EACH OTHER ARE SHADED (FARCTIONAL VALUE: 2 OUT OF 4)

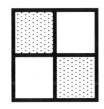  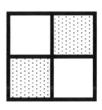

4 -PARTS. 2 PARTS DIAGONALLY ACROSS ARE SHADED (FARCTIONAL VALUE: 2 OUT OF 4)

HALF OF THE FIGURE IS SHADED (FARCTIONAL VALUE: HALF (OR) 1 OUT OF 2)

PARTS

  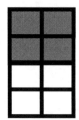

PARTS BY CUTTING SIDES

PARTS BY CUTTING CORNERS

ARROWS / LINES

ONE HEADED

ARROW

TWO HEADED

ARROW

THREE

ONE HEADED

FOUR HEADED

ARROW

| LINE | LINE WITH ONE END POINT | LINE WITH TWO END POINTS (Line Segment) |

CLASSIFICATION

Similar

in

COLOR

FIGURE CLASSIFICATION

HOW TO SOLVE?

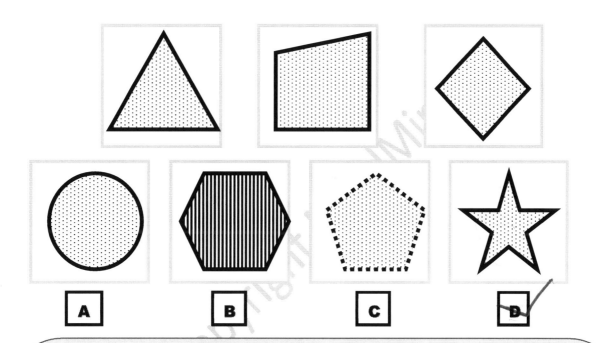

STEP#1: Understand how THREE figures are similar. All THREE figures must have something in common.

ALL FIGURES HAVE SOME NUMBER OF SIDES AND DOTTED PATTERN INSIDE.

ANSWER IS "D" (**HAS SIDES AND SAME DOTTED PATTERN INSIDE**).

A is incorrect. Pattern is same. But has no sides.

C is incorrect. Pattern is same. But Outline is incorrect

COLOR

1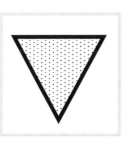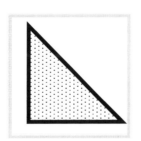

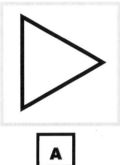   

 A B C D

2

 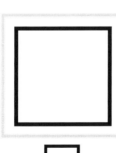 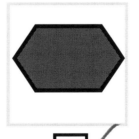 

A B C D

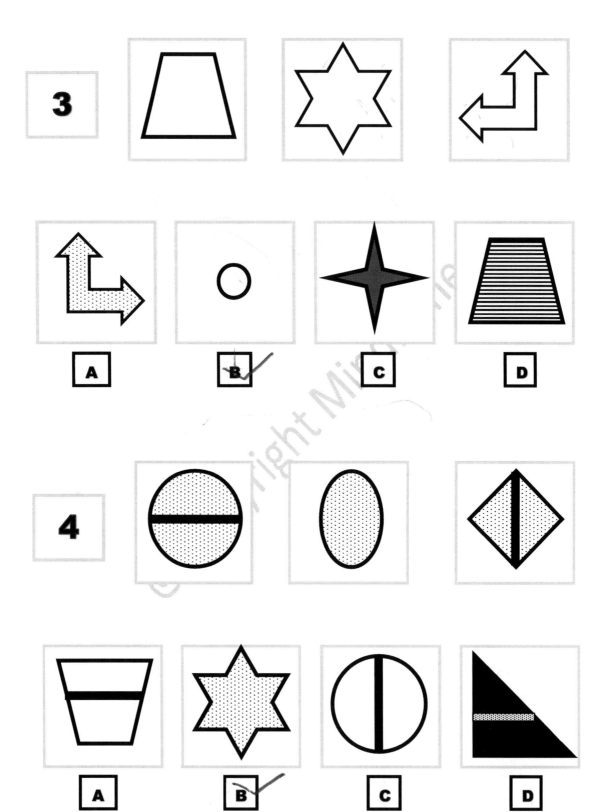

5

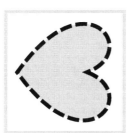  

 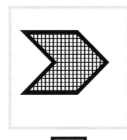 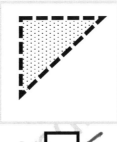 

 A B C D

6

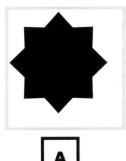 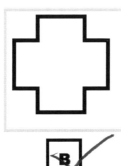 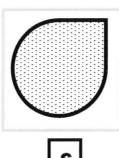 

 A B C D

7

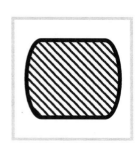 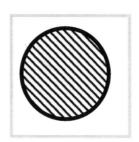 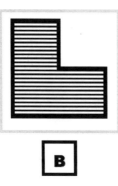

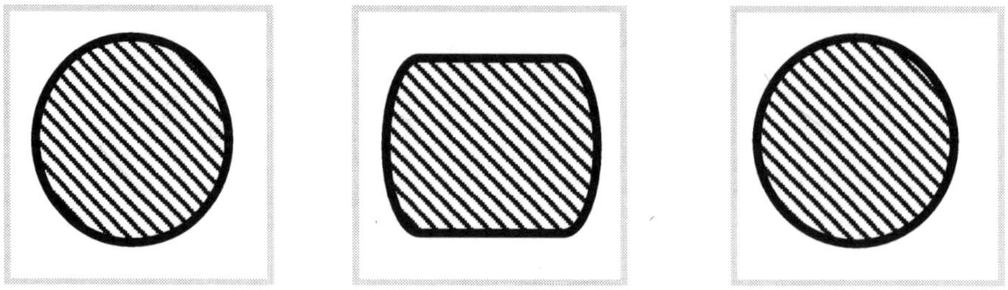

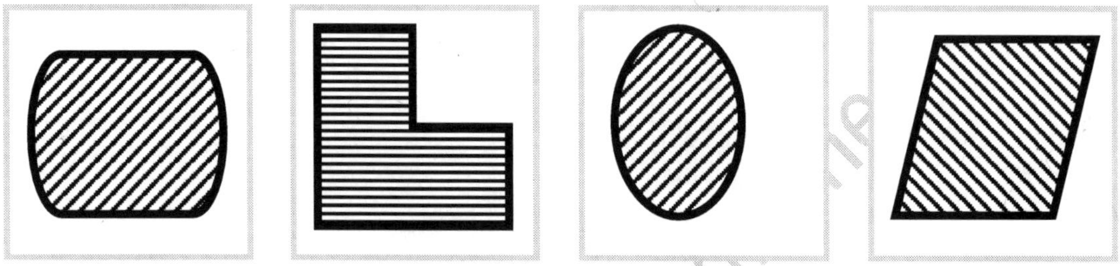

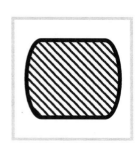 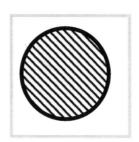

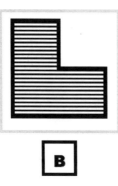 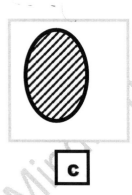 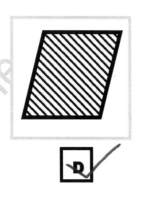

A	B	C	D

8

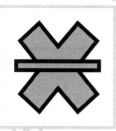 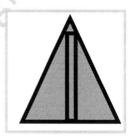 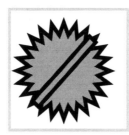

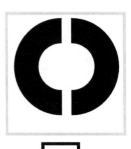 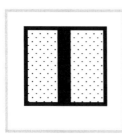 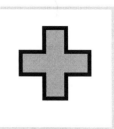 

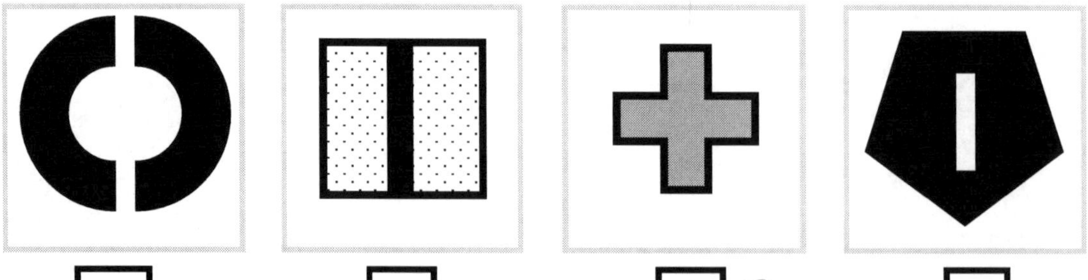

A	B	C	D

9

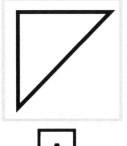  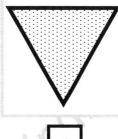 

| A | B | C | D |

10

 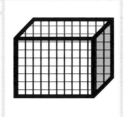 

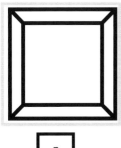 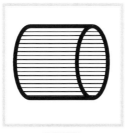 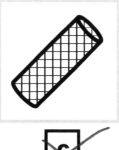 

| A | B | C | D |

11

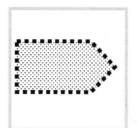  

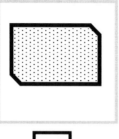  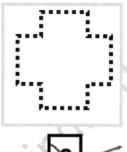 

A	B	C	D

12

 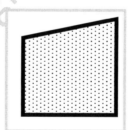 

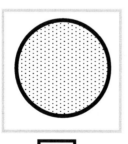 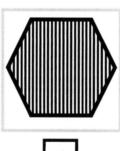 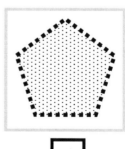 

A	B	C	D

13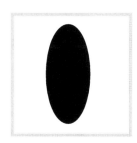

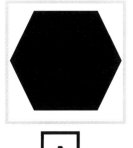   

A **B** **C** **D**

14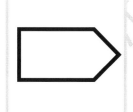

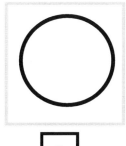  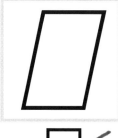 

A **B** **C** **D**

29

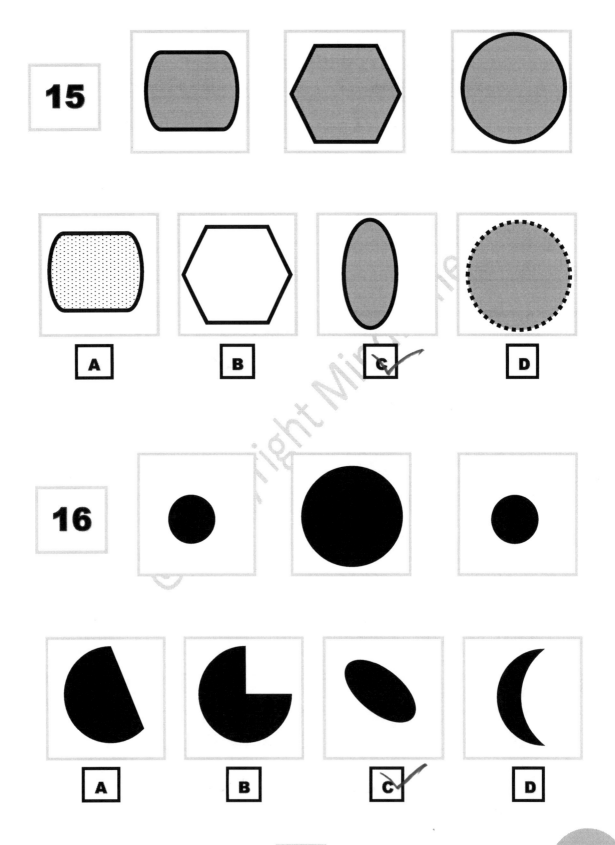

15

A | B | C | D

16

A | B | C | D

17

 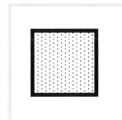 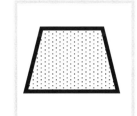

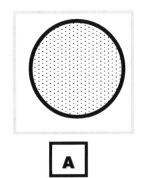 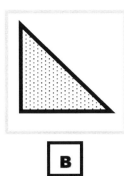 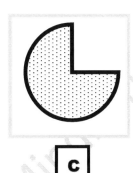 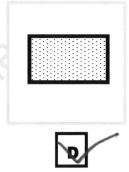

A   **B**   **C**   **D**

18

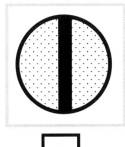 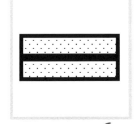  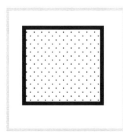

A   **B**   **C**   **D**

19

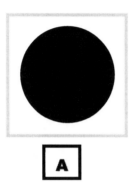 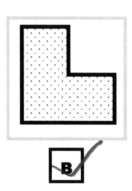 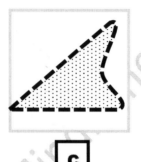 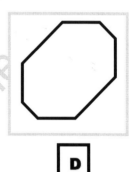

A **B** **C** **D**

20

 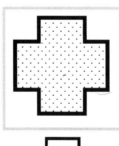  

A **B** **C** **D**

32

CLASSIFICATION

Similar

in

SHAPE

FIGURE CLASSIFICATION

HOW TO SOLVE?

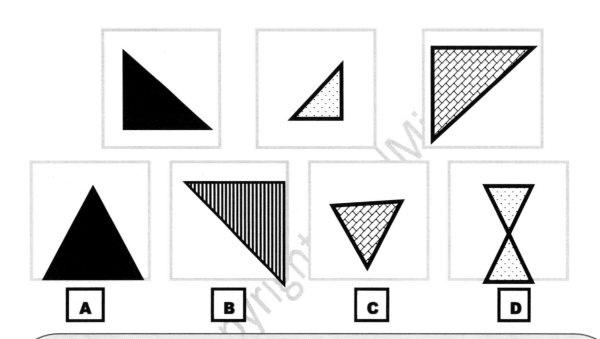

A B C D

STEP#1: Understand how THREE figures are similar. All THREE figures must have something in common.

ALL FIGURES ARE RIGHT ANGLE TRIANGLES

ANSWER IS **"B" (RIGHT ANGLED TRIANGLE)**

A is incorrect. It's an Equal sided Triangle

C is incorrect. It's an Equal sided Triangle

SHAPE

35

1

A B C D

2

A B C D

3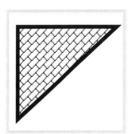

 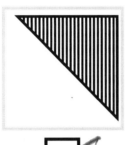  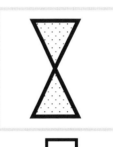

4

37

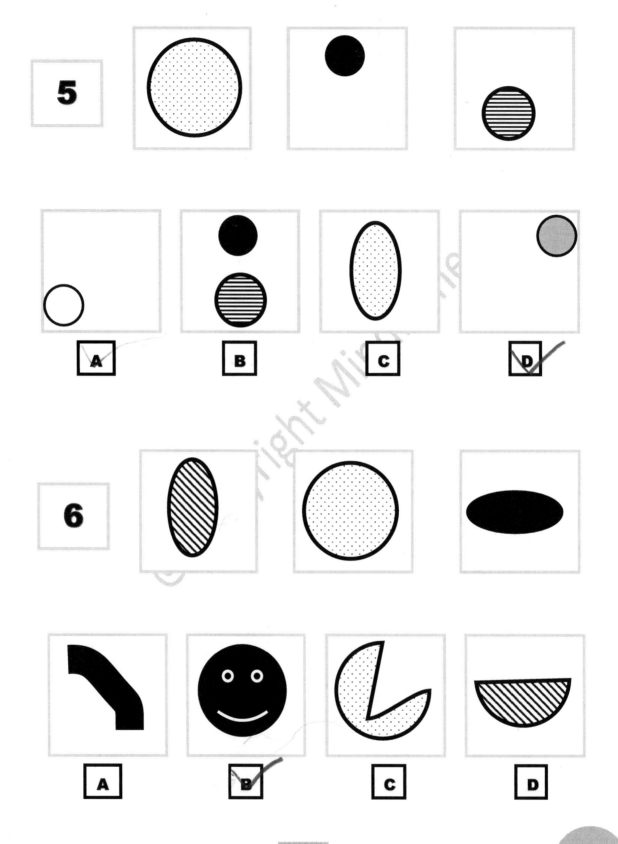

5

A   B   C   D ✓

6

A   B ✓   C   D

7

8

  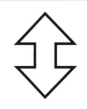

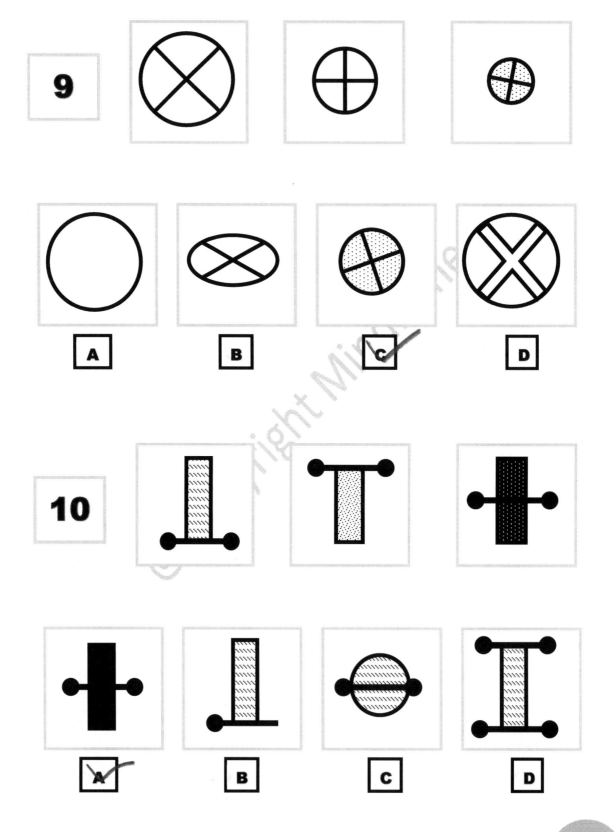

11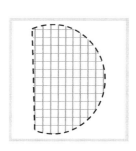

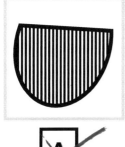  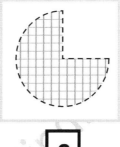 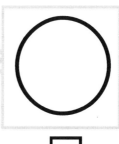

 A   B   C   D

12

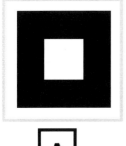 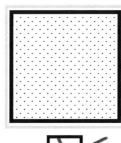 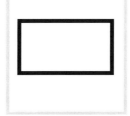 

A   B   C   D

41

13

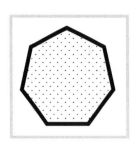 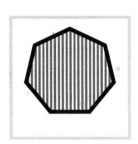 

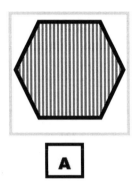   

 A B C D

14

  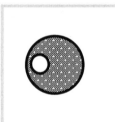

  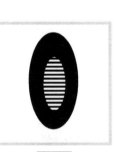 

 A B C D

15

A

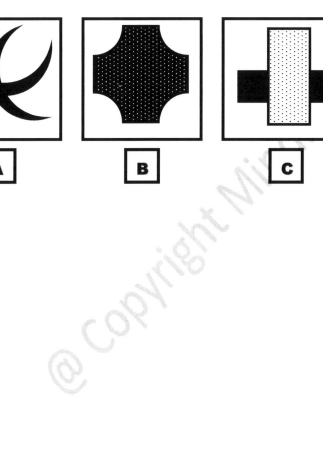

B

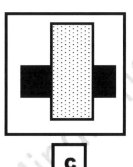

C

D

43

CLASSIFICATION

Similar in

NUMBER OF SIDES

FIGURE CLASSIFICATION

HOW TO SOLVE?

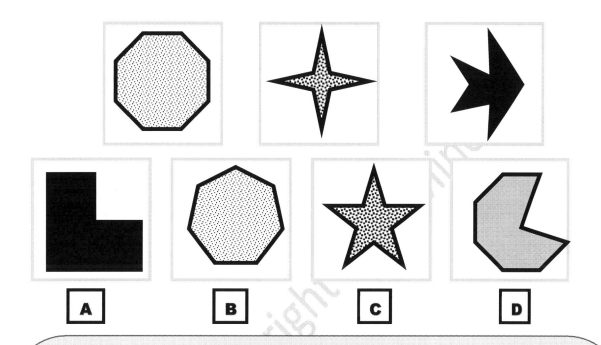

STEP#1: Understand how THREE figures are similar. All THREE figures must have something in common.

ALL FIGURES HAVE EIGHT SIDES

ANSWER IS **"D" (HAS EIGHT SIDES)**

A is incorrect. It has SIX sides

B is incorrect. It has SEVEN sides

C is incorrect. It has TEN sides

NUMBER OF SIDES

1

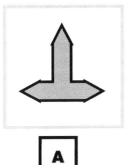 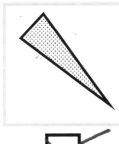  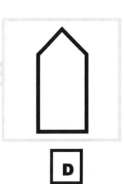

A B C D

2

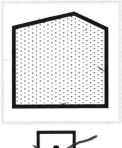  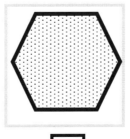 

A B C D

3

A	B	C	D

4

A	B	C	D

5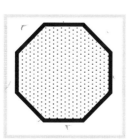

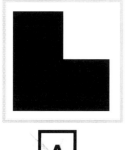 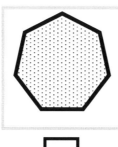  

 A B C D ✓

6

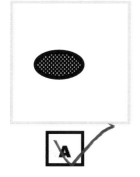   

 A ✓　B　C　D

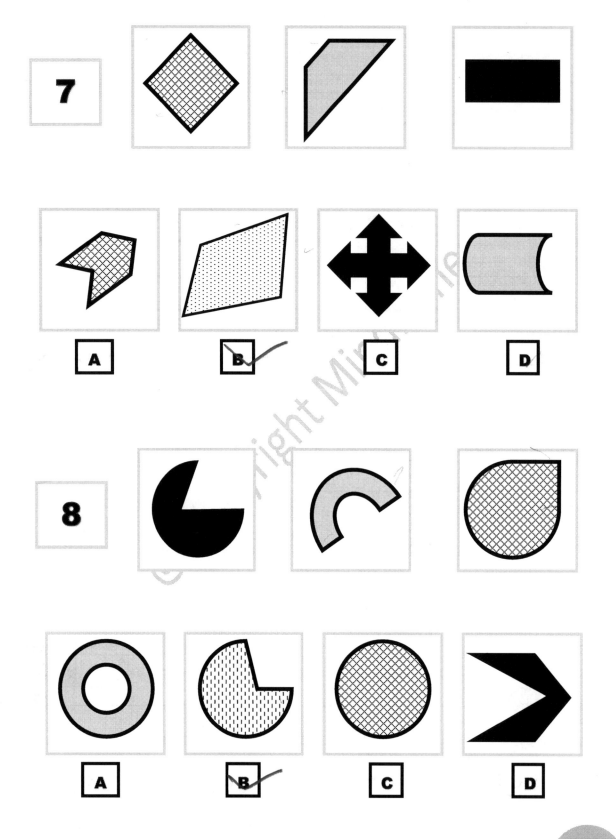

9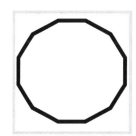

   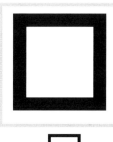

 A B | C | D

10

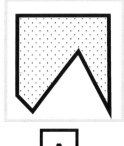 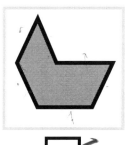 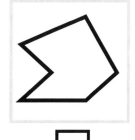 

 A B | C | D

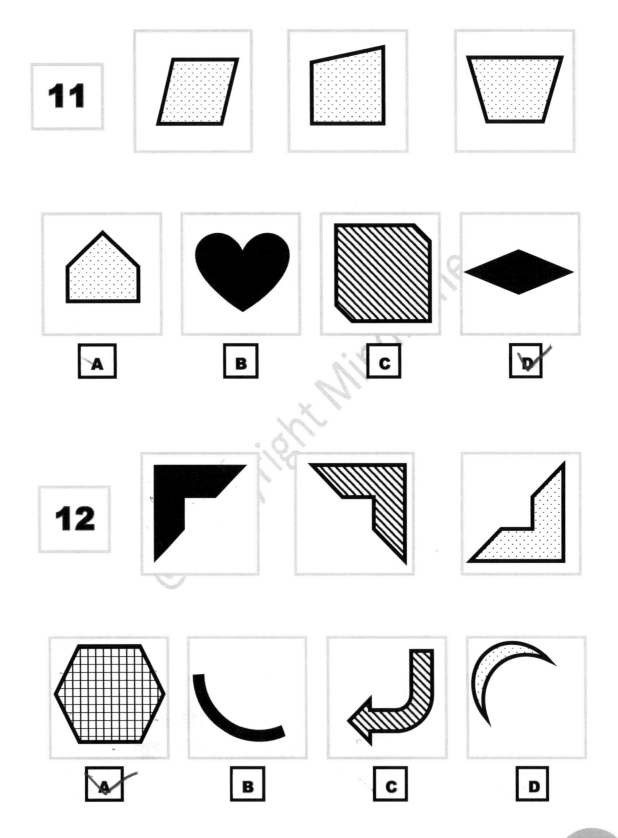

11

| A | B | C | D |

12

| A | B | C | D |

52

13

 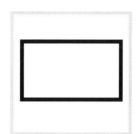 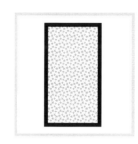

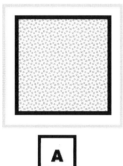  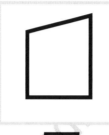 

 A   B   C   D

14

  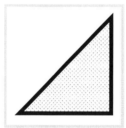

 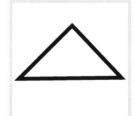  

A   B   C   D

15

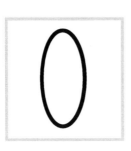 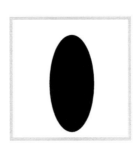 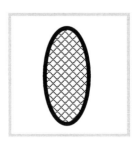

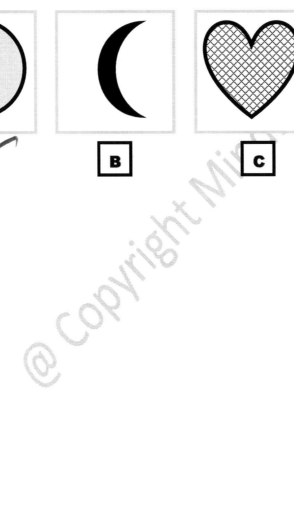

A B C D

CLASSIFICATION

Similar

in

NUMBER OF PARTS

Or

FRACTIONAL VALUE

FIGURE CLASSIFICATION

HOW TO SOLVE?

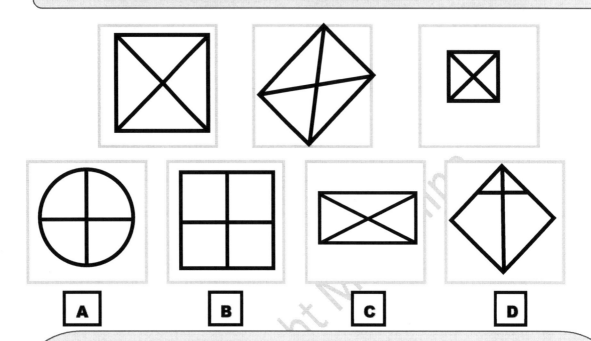

STEP#1: Understand how THREE figures are similar. All THREE figures must have something in common.

ALL FIGURES HAVE FOUR EQUAL PARTS WITH DIVIDING LINES FROM CORNER TO CORNER.

ANSWER IS "C" **(ALL HAVE 4 EQUAL PARTS WITH LINES DIVIDING CORNER TO CORNER)**

A is incorrect. It has 4 Equal Parts, but NO CORNERS

B is incorrect. It has 4 Equal Parts, but dividing lines are from side to side

D is incorrect. Parts are not of EQUAL size

PARTS/FRACTIONS

1

A   B   C   D

2

A   B   C   D

3

Options:
A   B   C   D

4

Options:
A   B   C   D

5

A B C D

6

A B C D

7

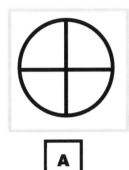 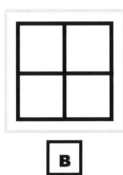  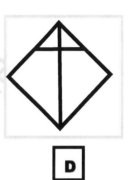

A B C D

8

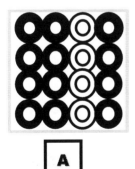 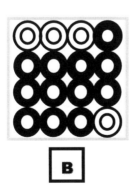 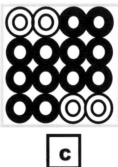 

A B C D

61

9

| A | B | C | D |

10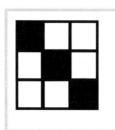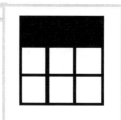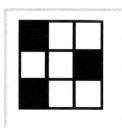

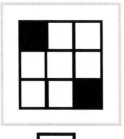 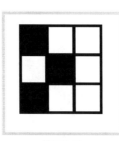 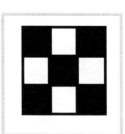 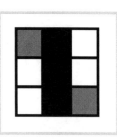

| A | B | C | D |

11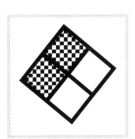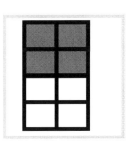

 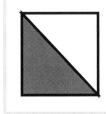 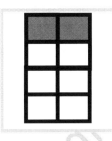 

A	B	C	D

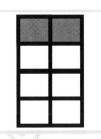  

12

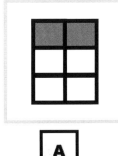 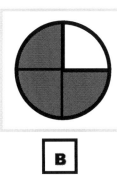 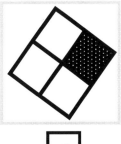 

A	B	C	D

63

13

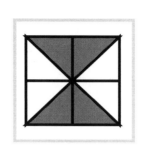  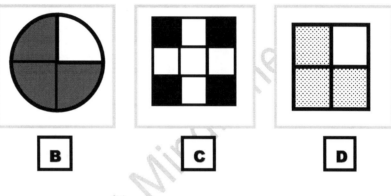

  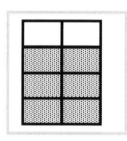

| A | B | C | D |

14

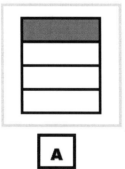   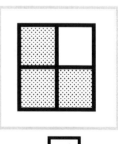

| A | B | C | D |

64

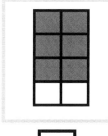

  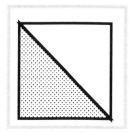

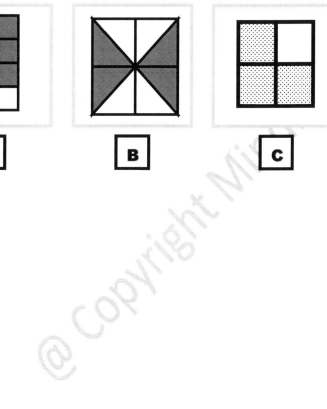

| A | B | C | D |

CLASSIFICATION

Similar

in

NUMBER OF FIGURES

FIGURE CLASSIFICATION

HOW TO SOLVE?

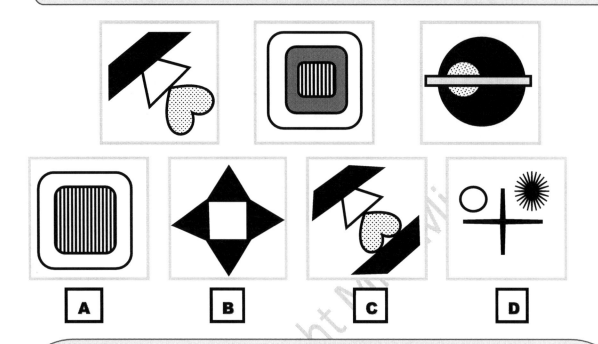

STEP#1: Understand how THREE figures are similar. All THREE figures must have something in common.

ALL HAVE THREE FIGURES.

ANSWER IS "**D**" (**ALL HAVE 3 FIGURES**).

A is incorrect. It has 2 Figures.

B is incorrect. It has 4 Figures.

C is incorrect. It has 4 Figures.

COUNT
(NUMBER OF FIGURES)

1

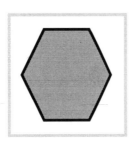 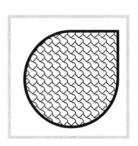 

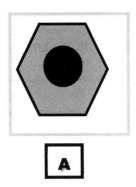  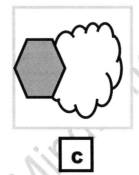 

A   B   C   D

2

 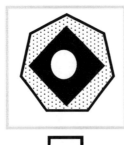 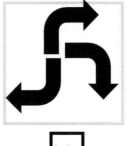 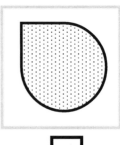

A   B   C   D

70

3

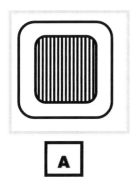

A

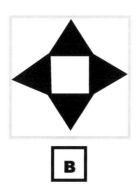

B

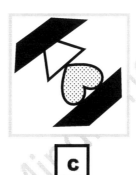

C

D

4

  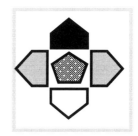

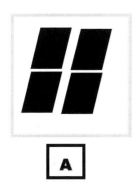

A

B

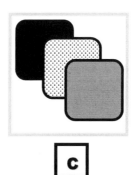

C

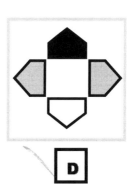

D

  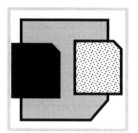

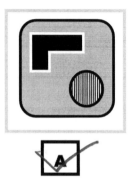 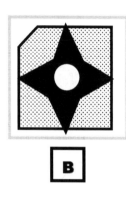  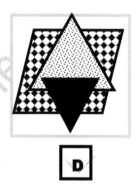

A   B   C   D

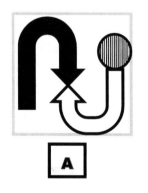  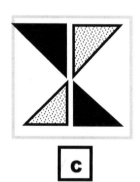 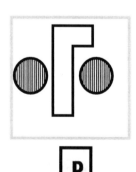

A   B   C   D

7

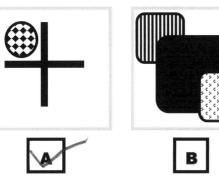

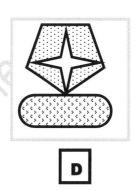

A ✓   **B**   **C**   **D**

8

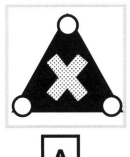   

A   **B**   **C**   **D** ✓

9

  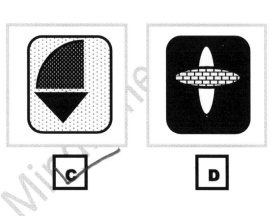

A	B	C	D

10

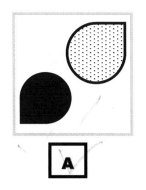 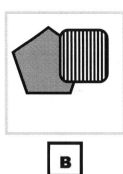 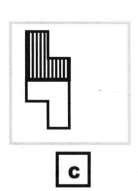 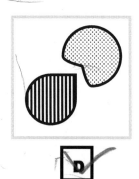

A	B	C	D

11

 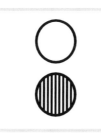 

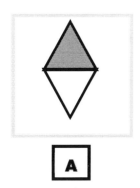  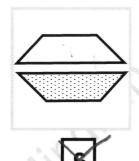 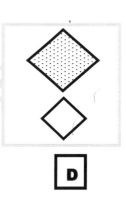

A	B	C	D

12

A	B	C	D

13

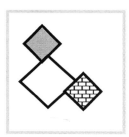  

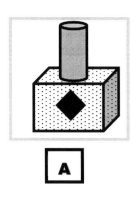 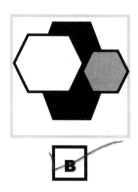  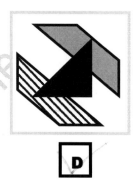

 A   **B**   **C**   **D**

14

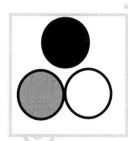  

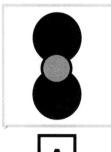   

A   **B**   **C**   **D**

15

 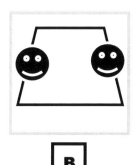 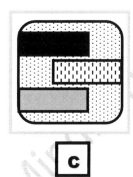 

A **B** **C** **D**

16

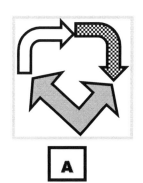  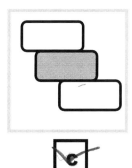 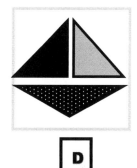

A **B** **C** **D**

17

  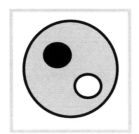

A	B	C	D

18

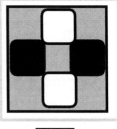   

A	B	C	D

19

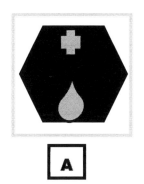 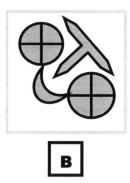 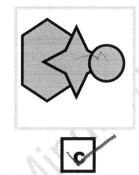 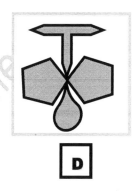

A   **B**   **C**   **D**

20

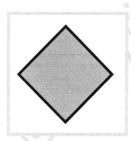 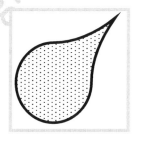 

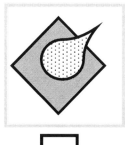   

A   **B**   **C**   **D**

CLASSIFICATION

SAME

or

TURNED

FIGURE CLASSIFICATION

HOW TO SOLVE?

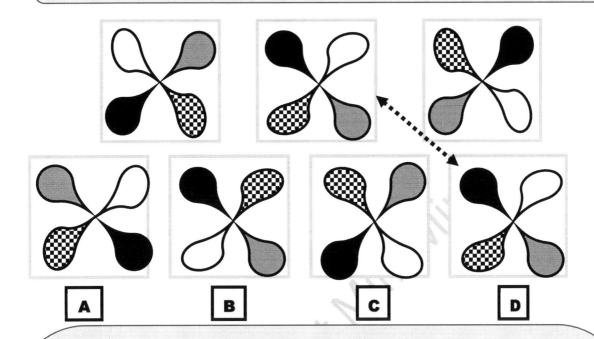

STEP#1: Understand how THREE figures are similar. All THREE figures must have something in common.

Figure in D MATCHES with Figure in 2ⁿᵈ Box

ANSWER IS "D" (**EXACTLY MATCHES WITH FIGURE IN 2ᴺᴰ BOX**).

A is incorrect. Figure is NOT same. Order of colors is NOT Same.

B is incorrect. Figure is NOT same. Order of colors is NOT Same.

C is incorrect. Figure is NOT same. Order of colors is NOT Same.

FIGURE CLASSIFICATION

HOW TO SOLVE?

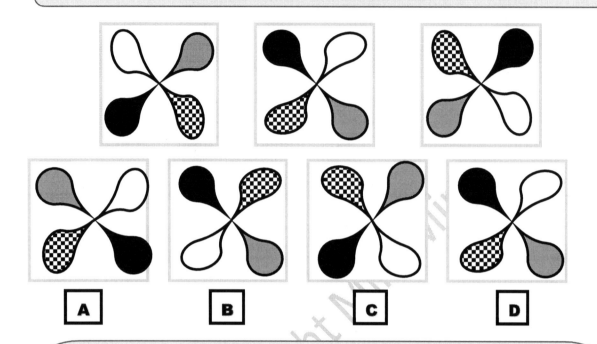

STEP#1: Understand how THREE figures are similar. All THREE figures must have something in common.

SAME FIGURE TURNED. ORDER OF COLORS IS SAME.

ANSWER IS "D" (**SAME FIGURE TURNED. ORDER OF COLORS IS SAME, CLOCKWISE: BLACK, WHITE, GRAY, PATTERN**).

A, B and C are incorrect.

Order of Colors for A, B, C is incorrect. Incorrect Order is: BLACK, PATTERN, GRAY, WHITE.

SAME or TURNED

1

  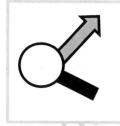 

A **B** **C** **D**

2

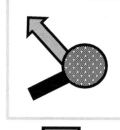  

A **B** **C** **D**

3

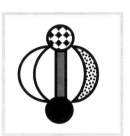  

 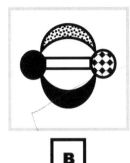 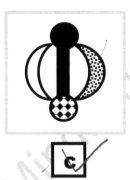 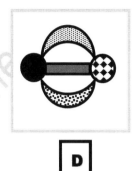

A   **B**   **C**   **D**

4

A   **B**   **C**   **D**

5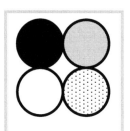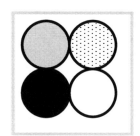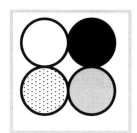

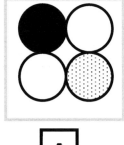 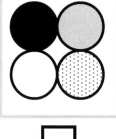 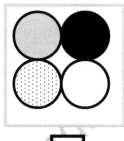 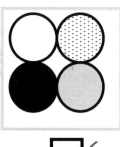

 A B C D

 6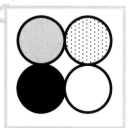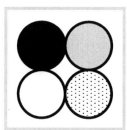

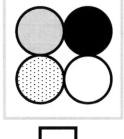 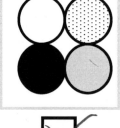 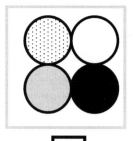 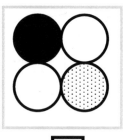

 A B C D

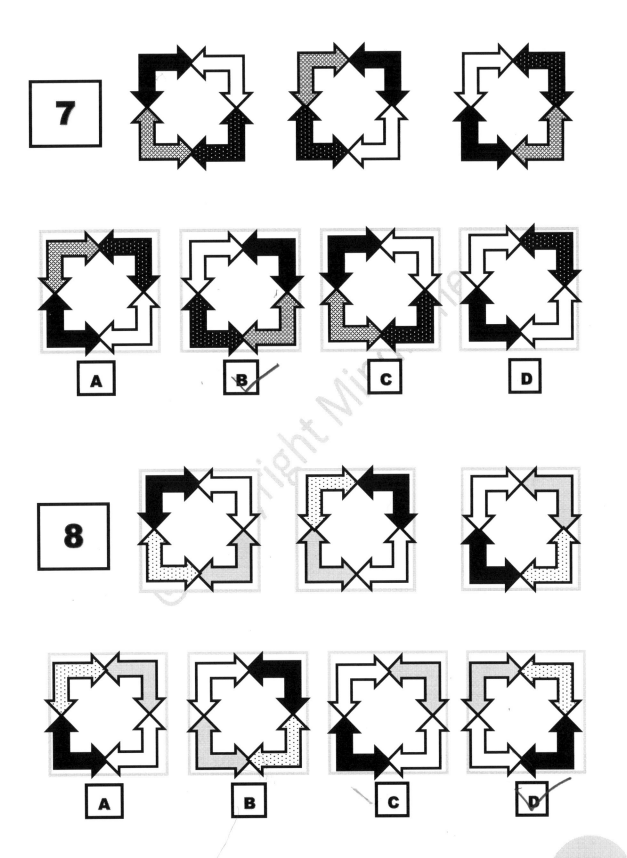

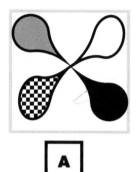 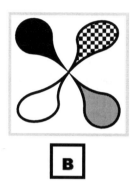 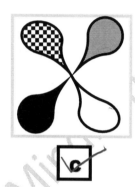 

A B C D

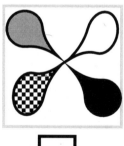 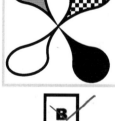  

A B C D

11

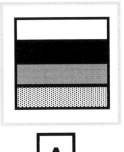 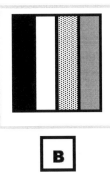 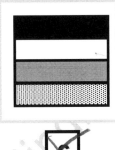 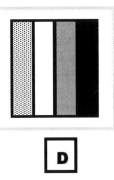

| A | B | C | D |

12

 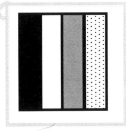 

| A | B | C | D |

13

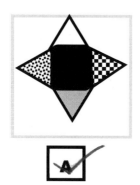 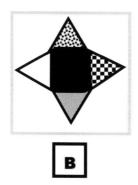 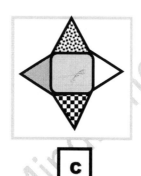 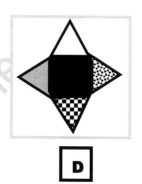

A **B** **C** **D**

14

 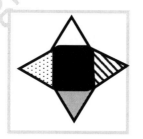 

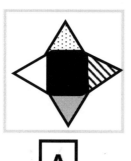 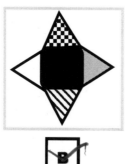  

A **B** **C** **D**

15

A

B

C

D

16

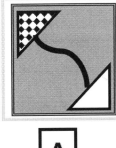
A

B

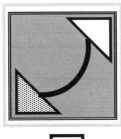
C

D

17

  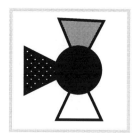

 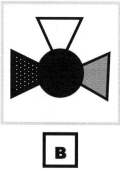  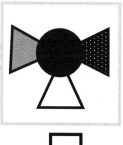

 A   B   C   D

18

 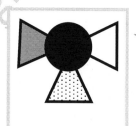 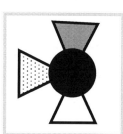

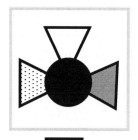 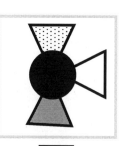 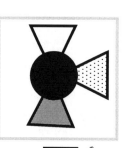 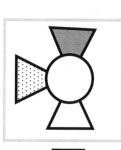

A   B   C   D

92

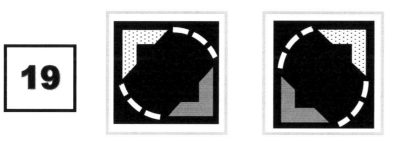

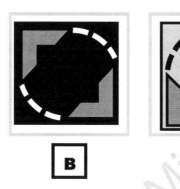
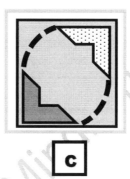
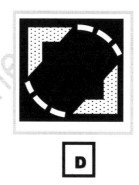

A **B** **C** **D**

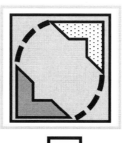

A **B** **C** **D**

21

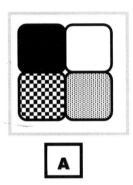 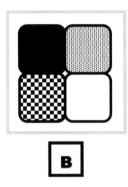 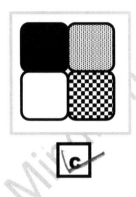 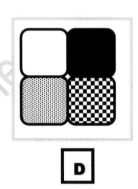

| A | B | C | D |

22

| A | B | C | D |

23

24

25

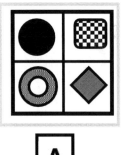 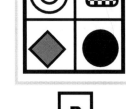  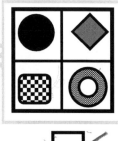

 A   B   C   D

26

 A   B   C   D

96

27

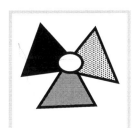 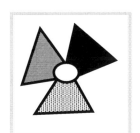 

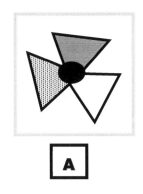 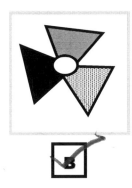 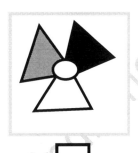 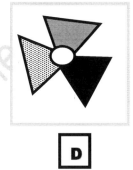

| A | B | C | D |

28

 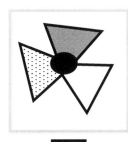  

| A | B | C | D |

29

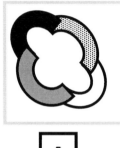  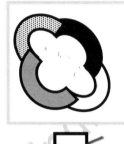 

A   B   C   D

30

A   B   C   D

98

CLASSIFICATION

LIST OF FEATURES

(Similar in Number, Shape, Color/Pattern but NOT necessarily Size, Order)

FIGURE CLASSIFICATION

HOW TO SOLVE?

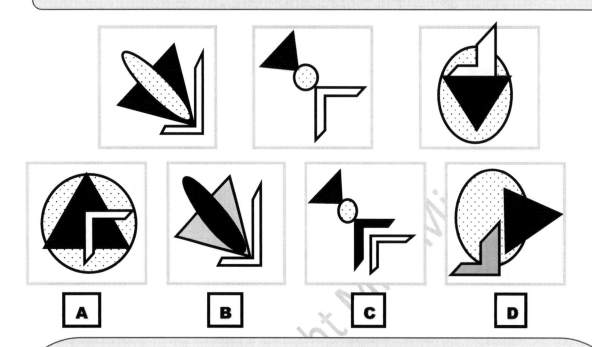

STEP#1: Understand how THREE figures are similar. All THREE figures must have something in common.

ALL HAVE 3 FIGURES. LIST OF FIGURES/FEATURES:

- **BLACK TRIANGLE**
- **DOTTED FIGURE WITH ZERO SIDES**
- **WHITE HALF FRAME**

ANSWER IS "A" **(MATCHES WITH THE LIST).**

B is incorrect. Triangle is Gray

C is incorrect. There are four figures

D is incorrect. Half Frame is GRAY

LIST

  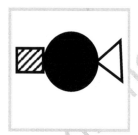 

A   **B**   **C**   **D**

  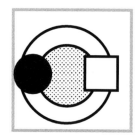

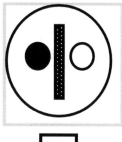 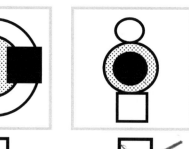 

A   **B**   **C**   **D**

102

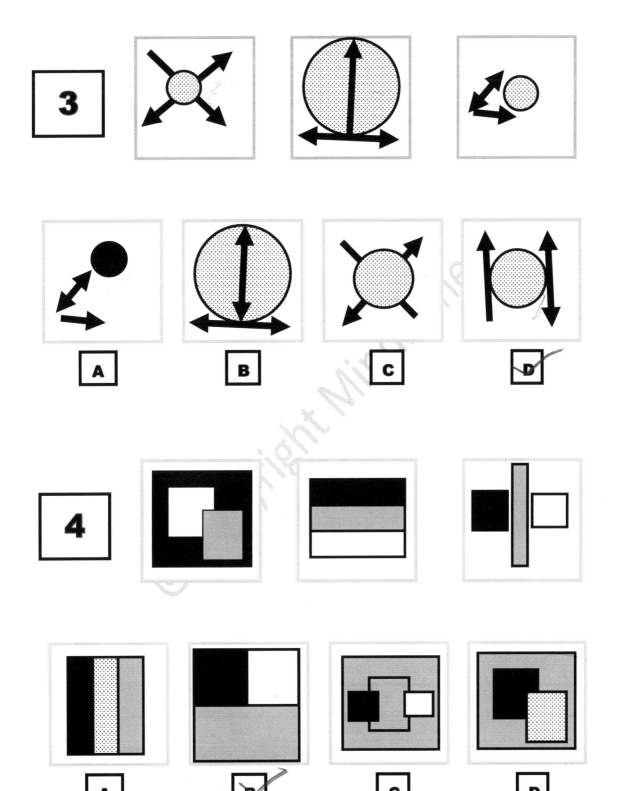

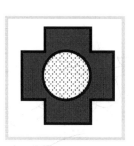  

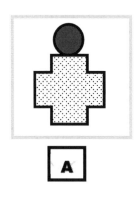 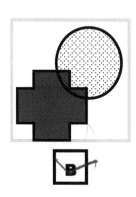 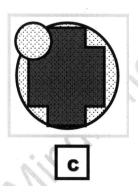 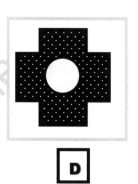

A B C D

  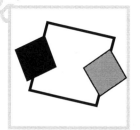 

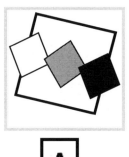 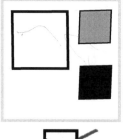 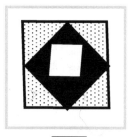 

A  B C D

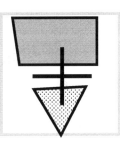

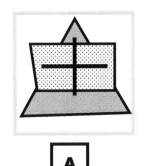
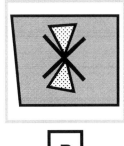
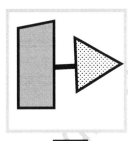
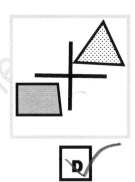

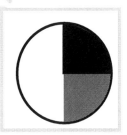

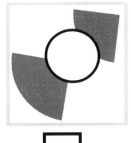

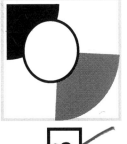

  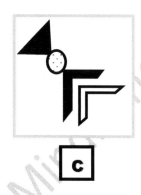 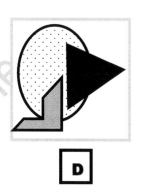

A B C D

 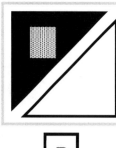  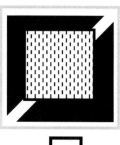

A B C D

A   B   C   D

A   B   C   D

13

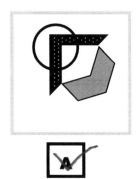 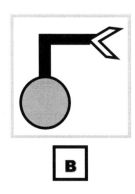  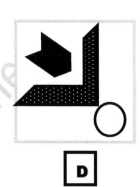

 B **C** **D**

14

A **B** **C** **D**

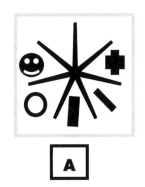   

A   B   C   D

A   B   C   D

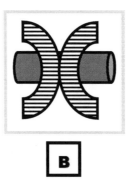

A **B** **C** **D**

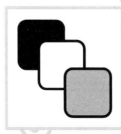 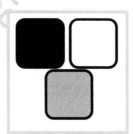 

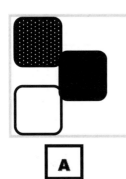

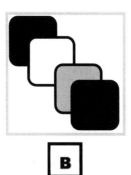

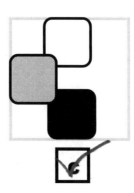

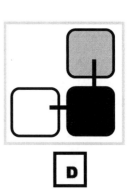

A **B** **C** **D**

 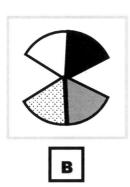 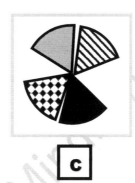 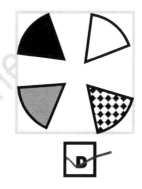

A **B** **C** **D**

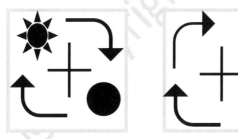  

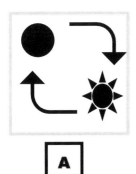 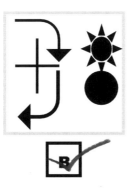 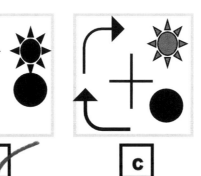 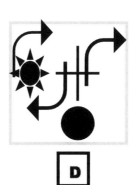

A **B** **C** **D**

FULL LENGTH
PRACTICE TEST - 1

1

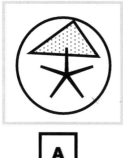   

2

   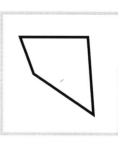

3

  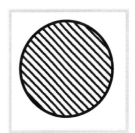

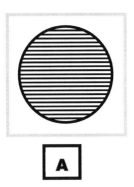 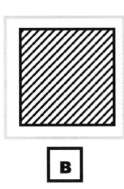  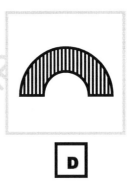

A **B** **C** **D**

4

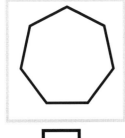  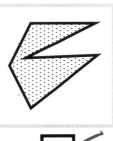 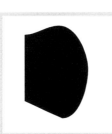

A **B** **C** **D**

5

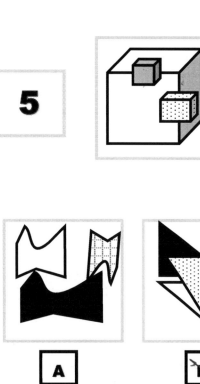  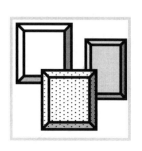

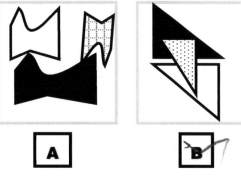 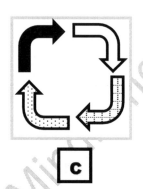 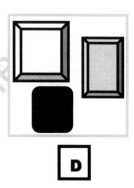

A   B   C   D

6

 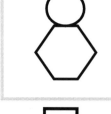  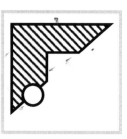

A   B   C   D

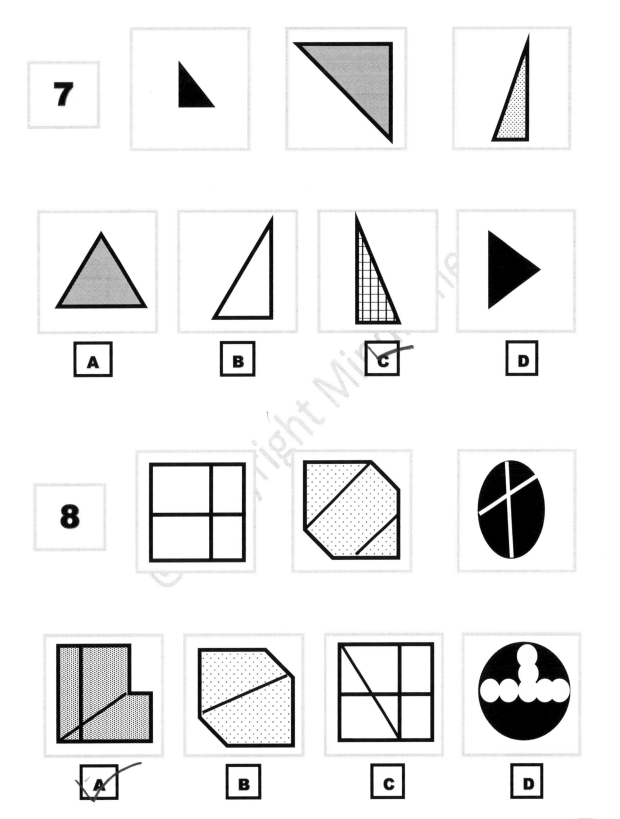

9

A B C D

10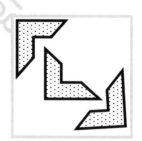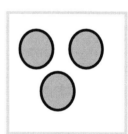

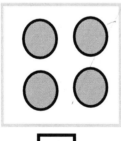 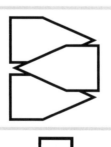 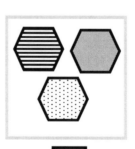 

A B C D

11

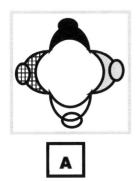 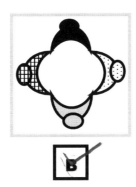 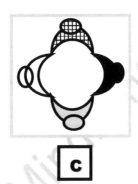 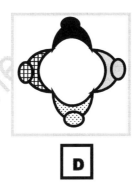

| A | B | C | D |

12

  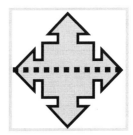

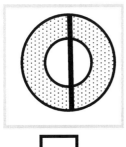   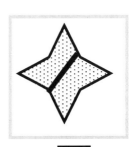

| A | B | C | D |

119

13

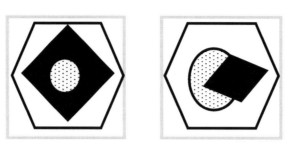 

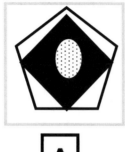 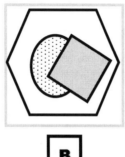  

A   B   C   D

14

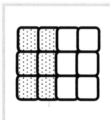 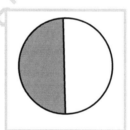 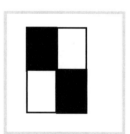

A   B   C   D

15

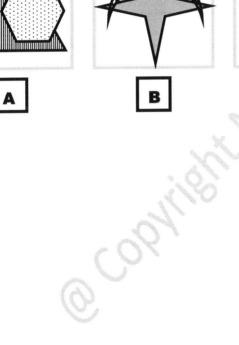 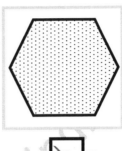 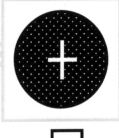

A **B** **C** **D**

FULL LENGTH

PRACTICE TEST - 2

A   B   C   D

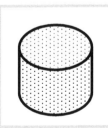 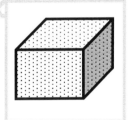 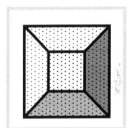

2

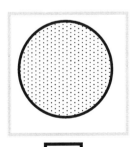   

A   B   C   D

123

3

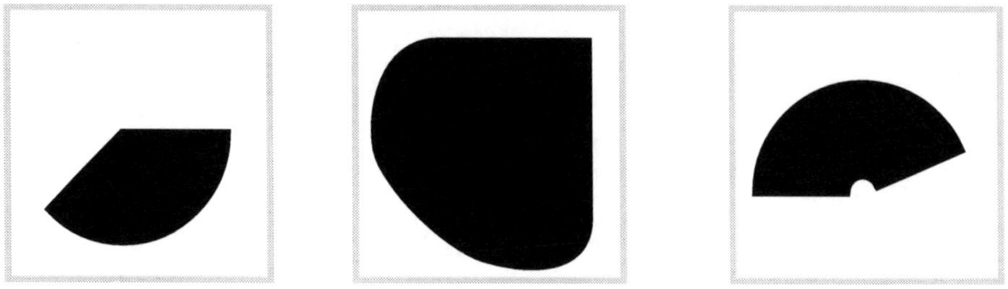

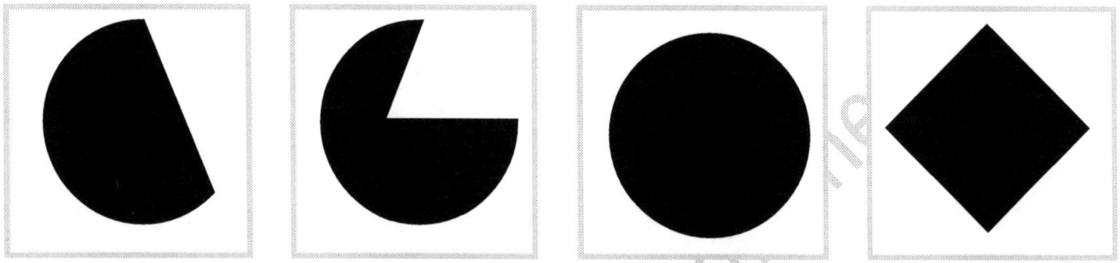

A

B

C

D

4

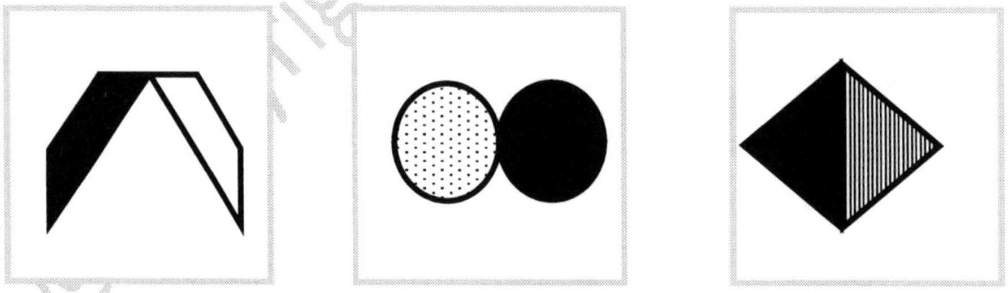

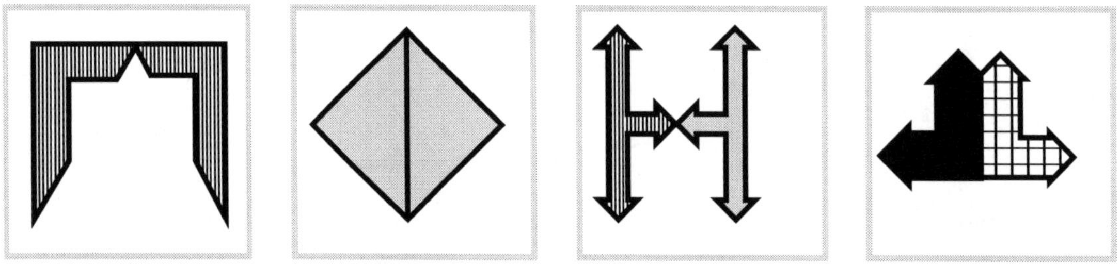

A

B

C

D

5

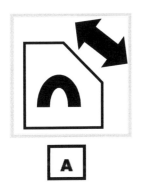
A

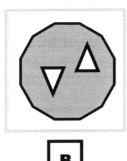
B

C

D

6

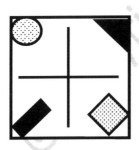 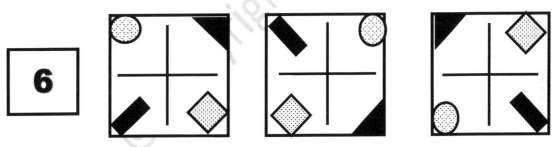 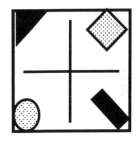

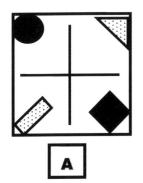
A

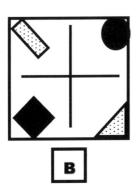
B

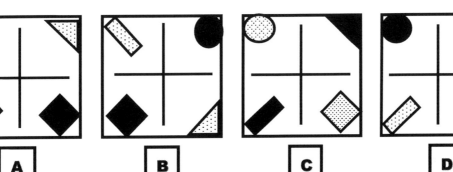
C

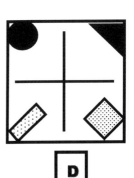
D

7

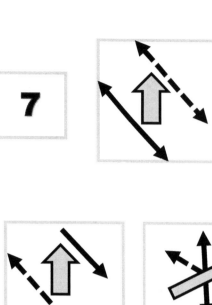 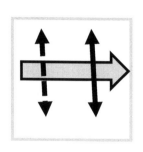 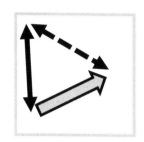

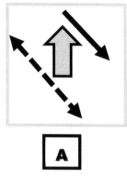 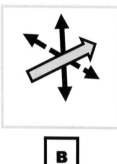 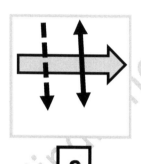 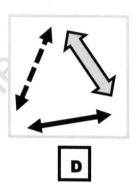

| A | B | C | D |

8

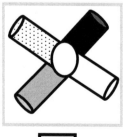   

| A | B | C | D |

126

9

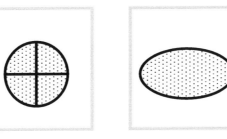 

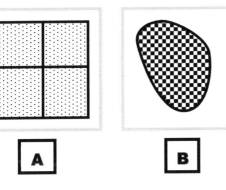

A

B

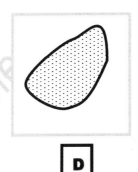

C

D

10

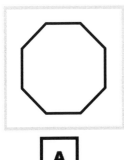

A

B

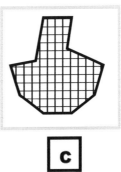

C

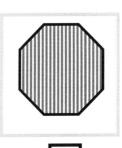

D

127

11

A   B   C   D

12

 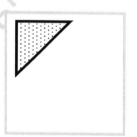 

 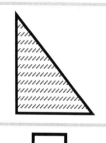 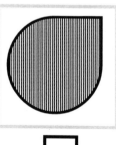 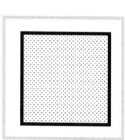

A   B   C   D

13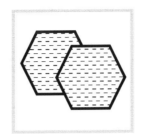

 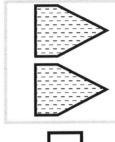  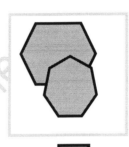

A   B   C   D

14

A   B   C   D

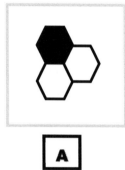

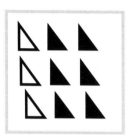  

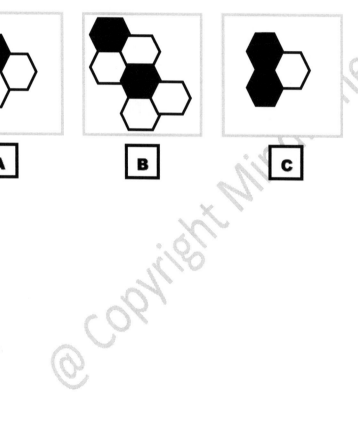

| A | B | C | D |

Mind Mine

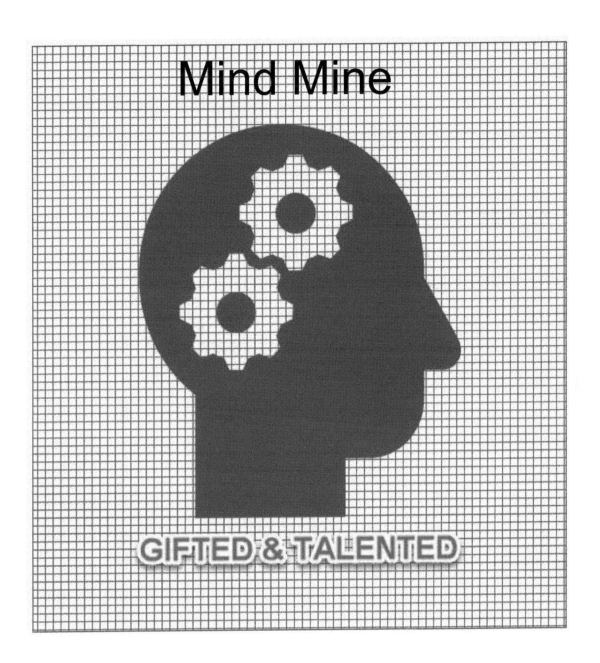

ANSWERS

Similar in COLOR

QUESTION #	ANSWER	CLASSIFICATION
1	B	Same pattern – Dots
2	C	Same color – Dark gray
3	B	Same color – White
4	B	Same pattern – Dots Black stripe is a distraction
5	C	Same outline – Dots
6	B	Same color – White
7	D	Same pattern – Diagonal lines from top left to bottom right
8	C	Same color – Gray
9	B	Same color – Black
10	C	Same pattern – Grid
11	D	Same outline – Dots All three figures have some color/pattern inside
12	D	Same pattern – Dots All figures have sides
13	C	Same color – Black

		All figures have ZERO sides
14	C	Same color – White All figures have sides
15	C	Same color – Gray
16	C	Same color – Black All figures have ZERO sides
17	D	Same pattern – Dots All figures have four sides
18	B	Same pattern – Dots All figures have four sides and one stripe inside
19	B	All figures have some number of sides with a solid outline and a pattern inside
20	B	Same pattern - Dots

Similar in SHAPE

QUESTION #	ANSWER	CLASSIFICATION
1	D	All figures are black triangles with equal sides
2	A	All figures are triangles with equal sides
3	B	All figures are right angle triangles
4	C	All figures are triangles
5	D	All figures have one circle with a fill pattern inside
6	B	All figures have ZERO sides
7	A	All figures are star-liked shapes
8	A	All figures are two-headed arrows
9	C	All figures have a circle with two intersecting lines
10	A	All figures have one rectangle with a two-pointed line (line segment)
11	A	All figures are part of a of a circle with one side
12	B	All figures are squares or diamonds
13	B	All figures have seven sides (septagons)

14	B	All figures are a circle with a smaller circle inside away from the center
15	D	All figures are a plus or an x shape

Similar in "Number of Sides"

QUESTION #	ANSWER	CLASSIFICATION
1	B	All figures have **3** sides
2	A	All figures have **5** sides
3	D	All figures have **5** sides
4	D	All figures have **6** sides
5	D	All figures have **8** sides
6	A	All figures have **0** sides
7	B	All figures have **4** sides
8	B	All figures have **2** sides
9	A	All figures have **12** sides
10	D	All figures have **7** sides
11	D	All figures have **4** sides
12	A	All figures have **6** sides
13	D	All figures are Rectangles

14	**B**	All figures are Right Angled Triangles
15	**A**	All figures have **0** sides

Similar in "Number of Parts or Fractional Value"

QUESTION #	ANSWER	CLASSIFICATION
1	B	One out of four parts is shaded
2	B	Two out of four parts are shaded
3	D	Two out of four parts are shaded, parts shaded are diagonally across
4	C	Two out of four parts are shaded, parts shaded are next to each other
5	C	All figures are cut into four parts with two intersecting lines
6	D	All figures have four sides and are divided into four parts with two intersecting lines
7	C	All figures have four equal parts with dividing lines from corner to corner
8	A	Four out of sixteen circles are white and consecutive
9	A	Two out of six parts are black
10	B	Three out of nine parts are shaded
11	B	Half the figure is shaded
12	C	One fourth of the figure is shaded

139

13	A	Half the figure is shaded
14	D	Three fourths of the figure is shaded
15	B	Half the figure is shaded

Similar in "Number of Figures"

QUESTION #	ANSWER	CLASSIFICATION
1	B	One figure in each box
2	A	Two figures in each box
3	D	Three figures in each box
4	B	Five figures in each box
5	B	Two figures inside a rectangular figure
6	B	Two figures in each box
7	A	Two figures in each box
8	D	One figure inside of another figure
9	C	Two non-overlapping figures inside a rounded square
10	D	Two non-overlapping figures, one with vertical lines
11	C	Two non-overlapping congruent figures that are flipped vertically
12	D	Two congruent figures that are side by side, touching each other and are flipped. One figure is black and the other has diagonal lines
13	B	Three similar figures

14	**C**	Three congruent figures
15	**A**	Two congruent figures inside a rounded square
16	**C**	Three congruent figures
17	**B**	Three similar figures
18	**D**	Four congruent figures inside a gray square
19	**C**	Three gray figures
20	**C**	One figure in each box

Same Figure

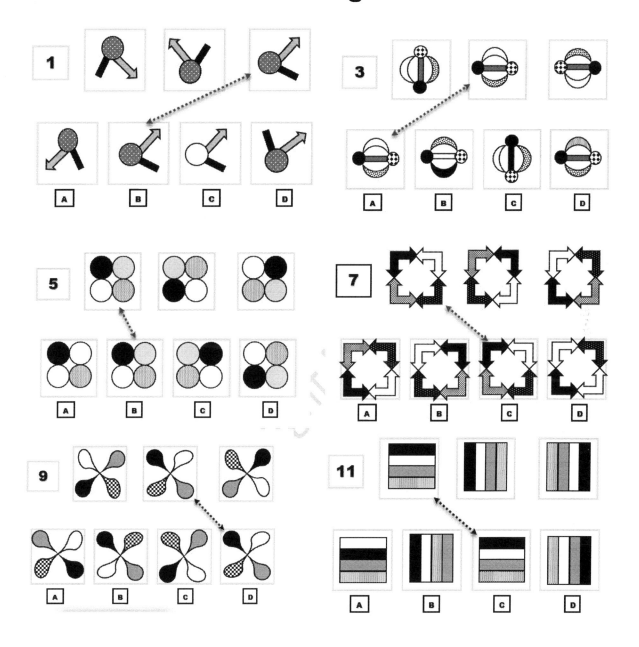

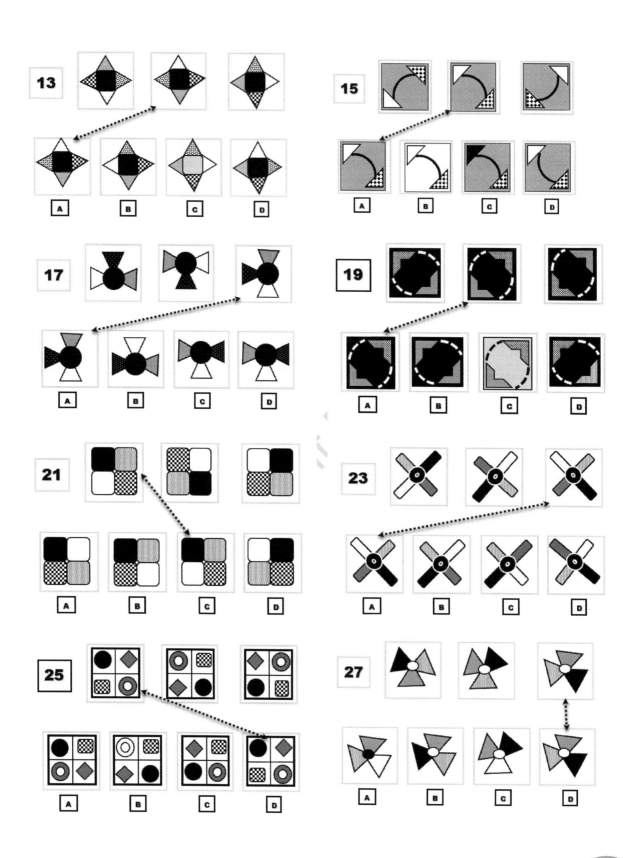

29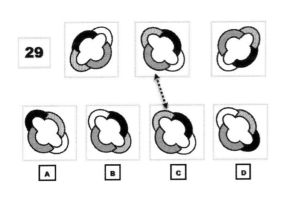

Same Figure or Turned

QUESTION #	ANSWER	CLASSIFICATION
1	B	Matches exactly with figure in 3rd box
2	D	Same figure turned. Order of colors is same, clockwise: Gray arrow Black rectangle
3	A	Matches exactly with figure in 2nd box
4	C	Same figure turned. Order of colors is same, clockwise: Soccer ball Dotted crescent Black circle White crescent
5	B	Matches exactly with figure in 1st box
6	C	Same figure turned. Order of colors is same, clockwise: Black circle Gray circle Dotted circle White circle
7	C	Matches exactly with figure in 1st box
8	D	Same figure turned. Order of colors is same, clockwise: Black arrow White arrow Gray arrow Dotted arrow

146

9	D	Matches exactly with figure in 2nd box
10	B	Same figure turned. Order of colors is same, clockwise: White balloon Gray balloon Patterned balloon Black balloon
11	C	Matches exactly with figure in 1st box
12	D	Same figure turned. Order of colors is same, clockwise: Black Rectangle White Rectangle Gray Rectangle Dotted Pattern Rectangle
13	A	Matches exactly with figure in 2nd box
14	B	Same figure turned. Order of colors is same, clockwise: Gray Triangle Dotted Triangle White Triangle Triangle with lines
15	A	Matches exactly with figure in 2nd box
16	D	Same figure turned. Order of colors is same, clockwise: White Triangle Triangle with Pattern

17	A	Matches exactly with figure in 3rd box
18	C	Same figure turned. Order of colors is same, clockwise: White Triangle Dotted Pattern Triangle Gray Triangle
19	A	Matches exactly with figure in 2nd box
20	D	Same figure turned. Order of colors is same, clockwise: Dotted Pattern Figure White Arc Gray Figure White Arc
21	C	Matches exactly with figure in 1st box
22	B	Same figure turned. Order of colors is same, clockwise: Black square Dotted square Square with vertical lines White square
23	A	Matches exactly with figure in 3rd box
24	B	Same figure turned. Order of colors is same, clockwise: Dotted rectangle Black rectangle Gray rectangle White rectangle
25	D	Matches exactly with figure in 1st box

26	**C**	Same figure turned. Order of colors is same, clockwise: Black circle Gray diamond Patterned donut Checkered square
27	**D**	Matches exactly with figure in 3rd box
28	**A**	Same figure turned. Order of colors is same, clockwise: Black triangle Dotted triangle Gray triangle
29	**C**	Matches exactly with figure in 2nd box
30	**A**	Same figure turned. Order of colors is same, clockwise: Black arc White arc Gray arc Dotted arc

List of Features

QUESTION #	ANSWER	CLASSIFICATION
1	C	All have 3 figures. List of Figures/Features: • White triangle • Black circle • Four-sided figure with diagonal lines
2	C	All have 3 figures. List of Figures/Features: • White circle • Black circle • Dotted circle • White Four-sided figure
3	D	All have 3 figures. List of Figures/Features: • Dotted circle • One-headed arrow • Two-headed arrow
4	B	All have 3 figures. List of Figures/Features: • Black Four-sided figure • White Four-sided figure • Gray Four-sided figure
5	B	All have 3 figures. List of Figures/Features: • Patterned circle • Gray plus shaped figure
6	B	All have 3 figures. List of Figures/Features: • White Four-sided figure

		• Black Four-sided figure • Gray Four-sided figure
7	D	All have 3 figures. List of Figures/Features: • Gray Trapezium • Dotted Triangle • Two Intersecting Lines
8	C	All have 3 figures. List of Figures/Features: • Black Sector • Gray Sector • White Circle
9	A	All have 3 figures. List of Figures/Features: • Black Triangle • Dotted figure with zero sides • White Half Frame
10	A	All have 3 figures. List of Figures/Features: • Black Triangle • White Four-sided figure • Black Triangle
11	C	All have 3 figures. List of Figures/Features: • Black Star • Black Circle • Gray half-donut • Two Black Arcs
12	D	All have 3 figures. List of Figures/Features:

		• Dotted Plus shaped figure • White triangle • Black triangle • Gray triangle • Triangle with horizontal lines
13	A	All have 3 figures. List of Figures/Features: • White Circle • Gray Arrow head • Patterned Half-frame
14	C	All have 3 figures. List of Figures/Features: • Dotted Circle • Black Right-angled Triangle • Gray heart • Diamond with horizontal lines • Gray Circle with spikes
15	B	All have 3 figures. List of Figures/Features: • Black Star • Black Smiley • White Circle • Black Four-sided figure • Black Plus-shaped sign • Black Dotted line
16	C	All have 3 figures. List of Figures/Features: • Black Dumbbell • Black Matchstick • Gray Matchstick

17	A	All have 3 figures. List of Figures/Features: <ul><li>Half Donut with Vertical lines</li><li>Half Donut with Horizontal lines</li><li>Gray Cylinder</li></ul>
18	C	All have 3 figures. List of Figures/Features: <ul><li>Black Square</li><li>White Square</li><li>Gray Square</li></ul>
19	D	All have 3 figures. List of Figures/Features: <ul><li>Checkered Triangle</li><li>White Triangle</li><li>Black Triangle</li><li>Gray Triangle</li></ul>
20	B	All have 3 figures. List of Figures/Features: <ul><li>Black Sun</li><li>Plus-shaped Sign</li><li>Two Bent Arrows</li><li>Black Circle</li></ul>

FULL LENGTH PRACTICE TEST#1

QUESTION #	ANSWER	CLASSIFICATION
1	D	• Three figures in each box. • One of these figures must be a Black circle.
2	A	• All figures are trapeziums (four sides). • All figures are filled with either color or pattern.
3	C	• All figures have same pattern – Diagonal lines from top left to bottom right.
4	C	• All figures have six sides.
5	B	• Three similar figures in each box. • One of these figures must have dotted pattern
6	D	• Two figures in each box. • One of these figures must be a figure with no sides (zero sides). • The other figure has six sides and is filled with either color or pattern.

7	C	• Right Angled triangles filled with either color or pattern.
8	A	• One figure with two lines inside.
9	C	• Same figure turned. • Order of colors is same, clockwise: Black Arrow, Gray Arrow, White Arrow.
10	D	• Three congruent figures in each box. • All three figures are filled with either same color or same pattern.
11	B	• Same figure turned. • Order of colors is same, clockwise: Dots, Gray, Grid, Black.
12	D	• One figure with sides and with a line inside the figure.
13	D	• 2 figures inside a white hexagon. List of figures/features inside the hexagon: ○ One black four-sided figure

		○ One figure with no sides (zero sides) and dots inside
14	A	• Half of the figure is shaded/filled.
15	C	• One figure in each box

FULL LENGTH PRACTICE TEST#2

QUESTION #	ANSWER	CLASSIFICATION
1	B	• Same figure turned. • Order of colors is same, clockwise: white, Gray, Black, patterned.
2	C	• Solid(3D) figures with dotted pattern
3	B	• All figures have two sides and are black
4	D	• Two congruent figures that are side by side, touching each other and are flipped. One of the figures is black.

5	D	• All have 3 figures. Color of Figures:
		   • White color
		   • Gray color
		   • Black color

6	C	• Matches exactly with figure in 1st Box. --- Alternatively ---- • Order of figures is same, clockwise: Dotted Circle, Black

		right-angled triangle, Dotted diamond, Black rectangle.

7	B	• All have 3 figures.
		• List of Figures/Features:
		  • Two-headed solid arrow
		  • Two-headed dotted arrow
		  • One-headed Gray arrow

8	C	• Same figure turned. • Order of colors is same, clockwise: Black, Patterned, White, Gray.
9	D	• Figure with no sides (Zero sides) and dotted pattern
10	D	• All figures have 8 sides and are filled with either color or pattern.
11	D	• Matches exactly with figure in 2nd Box.
12	B	• All figures are right-angled triangles

13	C	• Two overlapping congruent figures
14	C	• All figures have 4 sides and with a white dotted line inside connecting two corners.
15	C	Two-thirds (2/3$^{rd)}$) of figures are shaded

Mini Practice Tests

Questions are organized by each individual concept. Picking 15 questions randomly and solving them out of order serve as a mini practice test. **About 10 mini practice tests** can be generated.

Additional Help

Have a question? You can reach author directly at **mindmineauthor@gmail.com**

Mind Mine

GIFTED & TALENTED

161

Made in the USA
Coppell, TX
09 September 2020

37113213R20092